This book belongs to:

____

____

____

Kwame and Kofi are twins and best of friends! Even though they got along so well, they couldn't be more different. Kofi was very chatty, he liked to play sports and do lots of exercise, whilst Kwame was quiet and shy, but he loved to make loud music!

When Kwame was in year five at school, he had the chance to try so many instruments. Kwame tried to play the piano, but the keys were too big for his small hands. He even tried to play violin just like his friend James, but it just was not for him!

He could not move his fingers around the strings easily and his family did not enjoy the high pitched squeaking sound he made when playing in the bedroom that he and Kofi shared.

Kwame decided he wanted to try
instruments from the woodwind family.
The bassoon, clarinet oboe and flute, but
his absolute favourite was the big shiny
saxophone!

Although it is made of brass - the wooden
reed on the mouth piece means
it is part of the woodwind family.

Kwame decided to learn all about the different types of saxophones. He grew to understand that the saxophone family had at least six differently sized instruments, and they all played notes at different pitches.

The small ones played notes that were very very high and the large ones played notes that were very very low - they almost made the ground shake!

Kwame learnt that to play notes on the saxophone, he had to press the buttons , called "keys", whilst he blew with all his might! The keys on every saxophone are in similar positions, which meant that Kwame could play them all.

Even though he liked all of them, Kwame loved the baritone and the alto saxophones the most. He borrowed one of each from his school.

For his birthday, Kwame's mother gave him his very own alto saxophone! He practised consistently for at least two hours every day!

With all that practice, his tone, the smoothness of the sound he made and the fluid style of the music improved so much!

13

Sometimes Kwame's friends and neighbours would come to his home to listen to him play. They sank into large sofas, perched on the rounded arms, relaxed on floor cushions and sat around the dining table in his home.

They would listen to him practising his pieces and they didn't mind if they heard the same song two or three times. They clapped and cheered enthusiastically when he had finished, it was great music to their ears!

well done!
that was amazing!

Over time, Kwame got better and better; soon he was asked to play at church and at school.

To get to the venues, he had to travel by bus. He would have so many instrument cases and bags of sheet music, that it would take him a little while to get everything in his grasp!

He took up so much space in the luggage rack, that other passengers thought he was going on holiday!

ST

Soon, lots of people had heard Kwame play at different locations and he left a good impression on them!

He would share his telephone number and Instagram handle. They messaged him and gave him the opportunity to play for even more people.

He played at beautiful weddings, sad funerals and uplifting christenings. He played in concerts with orchestras, jazz bands and as a soloist where he would be in the spotlight.

Kwame's brother Kofi went to university
in Wales and that meant Kwame had the
bedroom to himself and he stacked all
of his instruments and his music on the
shelves.

Music!

When it was time to choose a career Kwame
decided he would study music. He attended
the local Conservatoire to earn his degree.

The tutors and lecturers though he was great!
They helped him understand the technical
aspects of music and how to maintain his
instruments in tip-top condition.

Kwame is older now and is confident on many woodwind instruments. He has a car and can get all of the instruments inside it. He travels around the country to play at the different locations. This is so much easier than travelling by bus!

Kwame has become a superb saxophone
player because he realised quite quickly
that he needed to practise his instruments
every day.

He hopes to carry on playing for lots of
people around the world. He will travel as
far as Africa, Europe and America. Kofi
and all his family are very proud of him.

If you want to be a superb saxophonist, take a look at these references to learn how!

For Kids:

Kids Britannica
Kids Britannica page with an article introducing children to the basics of music.
https://kids.britannica.com/kids/article/music/399978

BBC Bitesize
Introduction to music based on your learning level
https://www.bbc.co.uk/bitesize/subjects/z9xhfg8

Let's Play Music
A child friendly introduction to learning how to read sheet music with easy to understand steps!
https://www.letsplaykidsmusic.com/how-to-read-music-made-easy/

Alto Sax Simulator
This game allows you to play many different virtual saxophones, try them all and see which one is your favourite!
https://scratch.mit.edu/projects/100486600/remixes/

<u>**For parents and guardians:**</u>

UCAS
Universities and Colleges Admissions Service (UCAS) guidance on
courses related to music as well as the entry requirements to get into
University and finance options for students.
https://www.ucas.com/explore/subjects/music

Conservatoires UK
"We represent the collective views of eleven UK conservatoires. Our role
is to develop best practice for training and education in the performing
arts and to promote the sector's excellence nationally and globally."
https://conservatoiresuk.ac.uk

Prospects
Information on musical education at a university level as well as future
job prospects following qualification.
*https://www.prospects.ac.uk/jobs-and-work-experience/job-sectors/creative-
arts-and-design/careers-in-music*

What do you want to be when you grow up? Draw it below!

Notes!

Check out some other books in the series!